CORE ADVAN

MW00889875

Making Sense of
Proportions

DR. RANDY PALISOC

IRONBOX®
Education

IRONBOX®
Education

Contents

Essential Background Information

Making Sense of Fractions

About the Author

My name is Dr. Randy Palisoc, and I'm on a mission to give kids **Power Over Numbers** and **Power Over Learning.**

I am a former classroom teacher, and I was a founder of the **five-time national award winning** Synergy Academies, whose elementary school was named the **#1 Urban Elementary School in America** by the National Center for Urban School Transformation in 2013.

The reason I designed this system is that too many students do not have a strong foundation in math, and they do not "get" the standard explanations found in many textbooks. This is troubling because students who struggle early on are often unable catch up to their peers later in life.

On the other hand, students who do have strong foundations have a greater shot at success later in life. In 2013, for example, students who were with Synergy since elementary school (all minority students) had a 95% pass rate on the California High School Exit Exam, compared to only about 79% statewide (all ethnicities).

As shown above, **strong foundations really do matter.**

The Core Advantage math fluency system by Ironbox Education is designed to build those foundations and to build fluency as quickly and as easily as possible. It does so by thinking like kids and teaching in a way that makes sense to them.

I designed this math fluency system based on my experience working with thousands of students from elementary school through high school and finding out what makes them successful. I hope you are able to use this system to give your students or children Power Over Numbers™ and Power Over Learning™!

google "randy palisoc ted talk"

Dr. Randy Palisoc received his Bachelor of Science degree from the University of Southern California (USC), his Master of Education degree from the University of California, Los Angeles (UCLA), and his Doctor of Education degree from USC.

Proportions Run Deep

Proportional relationships lay the groundwork for algebra.

Proportions cause great confusion for many students. This is troubling because proportions run deep into the heart of math, and they lay the foundation for algebra. For example, the following concepts all involve proportional relationships:

- **speed** (i.e., meters per second)
- **density** (grams per cubic centimeter)
- **concentration** (parts per million)
- **slope** (change in y per unit change in x)

As you an see, the better students understand proportions, they more easily they will grasp other algebraic concepts.

With this in mind, *Making Sense of Proportions* is designed to help students set up and see proportional relationships more easily. ***Making Sense of Proportions is a short but powerful unit, and you'll see how this unit uses proportions as a springboard to many other important concepts.***

Use the entire unit from beginning to end as designed, and students will come to appreciate proportions as a source of confidence and understanding instead of a cause of confusion.

How does this system work?

First things first.

In order to do keep up with this unit, students must be fluent with their multiplication and division facts. Additionally, students will be using fractions to express proportional relationships. Therefore, it is essential that students have successfully completed the following units first:

- *10 Powerful Steps to Multiplication Fluency*

- *Making Sense of Division*

- *Making Sense of Fractions*

The Core Advantage series is different from ordinary workbooks. The system is designed to have students work interactively on short, easy-to-understand guided lessons with their teacher or their parent. The reason for this is that when students (especially young students) work with an actual person, it makes learning a much more personal and meaningful experience. ***The human touch matters.***

It's important for teachers or parents to watch the lesson-by-lesson demo videos. This way, they'll know the key nuances to point out, and it takes the guesswork and confusion out of the lesson. There are also fully-annotated answer keys that not only show the answer, but also show the steps involved in getting there.

Each lesson provides students with well-thought-out, purposeful practice to promote fluency, and all the lessons build systematically upon each other. The following page provides a suggested pacing plan, and you can adjust the pacing as needed.

Pacing: Making Sense of Proportions

Proportions depend heavily on fractions, and fractions depend heavily on multiplication and division. Therefore, be sure students have gone through the following units before proceeding with this unit:

- 10 Powerful Steps to Multiplication Fluency
- Making Sense of Division
- Making Sense of Fractions

As mentioned earlier, proportions run deep and actually form the basis of many other mathematical concepts, including equations and graphing. Concepts that involve proportional relationships include:

- speed (i.e., meters per second)
- density (grams per cubic centimeter)
- concentration (parts per million)
- slope (change in y per unit change in x)

As a result, this short but powerful unit explicitly helps students make these connections clear using the sample two-week pacing below, which can be adjusted as necessary.

	Monday	Tuesday	Wednesday	Thursday	Friday
Week 1	Lesson 1 The Magic Formula for Proportions Lesson 2 Equivalent Fractions	Lessons 3 Setting Up and Solving Proportions Lessons 4 Setting Up and Solving Proportions	Lessons 5 Setting Up and Solving Proportions Lessons 6 Setting Up and Solving Proportions	Lessons 7 Setting Up and Solving Proportions: Speed Problems Lessons 8 Deriving the Speed Formula from a Proportion	Lesson 9 Graphing a Proportional Relationship Distance vs. Time Lesson 10 Graphing Distance vs. Time
Week 2	Lesson 11 Graphing Distance vs. Time Lesson 12 Graphing Distance vs. Time	Lesson 13 Calculating Distance with a Proportion in Disguise Lesson 14 Calculating Distance	Lesson 15 Graphing Distance vs. Time (Same Starting Point, Different Speeds) Lesson 16 Graphing Distance vs. Time (Same Speed, Different Starting Points)	Lessons 17 Calculating Distance with Changes in Units Lessons 18 Calculating Distance with Changes in Units	Lessons 19 Calculating Distance with Changes in Units Lessons 20 Calculating Distance with Changes in Units

Addressing State Learning Standards or the Common Core State Standards

Today, schools across America are either using their own state's learning standards or the Common Core State Standards.

No matter what learning standards a school is using, this system helps give students an academic advantage by building fluency faster than has been possible in the past. Fluency is important for all students because it helps them be more precise, which in turn helps them more easily make sense of math.

Take a look at these two Standards for Mathematical Practice (MP), which are used by states using the Common Core State Standards:

> MP #1: Make sense of problems and persevere in solving them.
> MP #6: Attend to precision.

How do these two math practices go together?

- If students **cannot** attend to precision (#6), then they will not make sense of problems (#1), and they will not persevere in solving them (#1).

On the other hand,

- If students **can** attend to precision (#6), then they are more likely to make sense of problems (#1) and are more likely to persevere in solving them (#1).

As you can see, attending to precision (#6) can mean the difference between confidence and confusion.

The unique Core Advantage system used in this book can help give students an academic advantage in a short amount of time. It is designed to build fluency so that students can attend to precision (#6) and actually understand what they're doing in math.

It does take hard work and practice on the part of students, and only students themselves can determine their level of success based on their effort. The good news is that the greater their level of fluency, the more confidence students will have, and the more likely they are to persevere and put in that necessary hard work and practice.

Fluency matters, and I hope that you are able to use this system to build that fluency with your students.

-- Dr. Randy Palisoc

Making Sense of Proportions | © MathFluency.com | **Teachers: Log in for demo videos.**

Name_____

Making Sense of
Proportions

Go down your **Success Tracker** in the order shown below, and write your score for each of the activities as you complete them. The goal is to make any corrections necessary to earn a score of 100%.

Unit	No.	Lesson Name	Score
Unit 1 What is a Proportion?	KEY LESSON 1	The Magic Formula for Proportions	
	KEY LESSON 2	Equivalent Fractions	
Unit 2 Setting Up and Solving Proportions	KEY LESSON 3	Setting Up and Solving Proportions	
	4	Setting Up and Solving Proportions	
	5	Setting Up and Solving Proportions	
	6	Setting Up and Solving Proportions	
Unit 3 Proportions Involving Speed	KEY LESSON 7	Setting Up and Solving Proportions: Speed Problems	
	KEY LESSON 8	Deriving the Speed Formula from a Proportion	
Unit 4 Graphing a Proportional Relationship	KEY LESSON 9	Graphing a Proportional Relationship: Distance vs. Time	
	KEY LESSON 10	Graphing Distance vs. Time	
	11	Graphing Distance vs. Time	
	12	Graphing Distance vs. Time	
Unit 5 $d = r \cdot t$ A Proportion in Disguise	KEY LESSON 13	Calculating Distance with a Proportion in Disguise	
	14	Calculating Distance	
Unit 6 Graphing Objects with Different Speeds and Different Starting Points	KEY LESSON 15	Graphing Distance vs. Time (Same Starting Point, Different Speeds)	
	KEY LESSON 16	Graphing Distance vs. Time (Same Speed, Different Starting Points)	
Unit 7 Calculating Distances with Changes in Units	KEY LESSON 17	Calculating Distance with Changes in Units	
	18	Calculating Distance with Changes in Units	
	19	Calculating Distance with Changes in Units	
	20	Calculating Distance with Changes in Units	

Making Sense of Proportions | © MathFluency.com | **Teachers: Log in for demo videos.**

Name_____

Lesson 1: The Magic Formula for Proportions

Directions: Follow along with your instructor to complete this lesson after watching the demo video.
Important Note: The smaller box and the the larger box are <u>proportional</u> to each other.

Smaller Box (representing the smaller photograph)

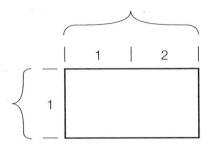

Larger Box (representing the larger photograph)

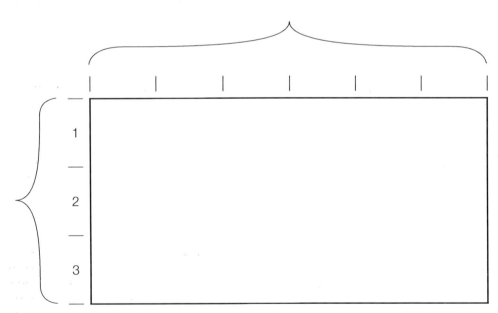

The Magic Formula

— = —

Use the Magic Formula to defend your answer from the demo.

— = —

Name_____

Lesson 2: Equivalent Fractions

Directions: Use multiplication or division to solve each equivalent fraction. Be sure to move from the "full" side to the "empty" side. Box your answer.

A. $\dfrac{3}{8} = \dfrac{15}{\quad}$	B. $\dfrac{16}{40} = \dfrac{2}{\quad}$	C. $\dfrac{10}{35} = \dfrac{\quad}{7}$	D. $\dfrac{1}{3} = \dfrac{\quad}{21}$
E. $\dfrac{18}{42} = \dfrac{\quad}{7}$	F. $\dfrac{5}{8} = \dfrac{\quad}{24}$	G. $\dfrac{3}{5} = \dfrac{24}{\quad}$	H. $\dfrac{36}{63} = \dfrac{4}{\quad}$
I. $\dfrac{12}{18} = \dfrac{\quad}{3}$	J. $\dfrac{25}{35} = \dfrac{5}{\quad}$	K. $\dfrac{4}{5} = \dfrac{8}{\quad}$	L. $\dfrac{6}{7} = \dfrac{\quad}{49}$
M. $\dfrac{1}{4} = \dfrac{\quad}{8}$	N. $\dfrac{1}{6} = \dfrac{4}{\quad}$	O. $\dfrac{1}{8} = \dfrac{\quad}{32}$	P. $\dfrac{9}{12} = \dfrac{3}{\quad}$
Q. $\dfrac{5}{\quad} = \dfrac{45}{54}$	R. $\dfrac{\quad}{8} = \dfrac{15}{40}$	S. $\dfrac{4}{\quad} = \dfrac{1}{5}$	T. $\dfrac{\quad}{7} = \dfrac{3}{21}$

Name_____

Lesson 3: Setting Up and Solving Proportions

$$\frac{\rule{1cm}{0.4pt}}{\rule{1cm}{0.4pt}} = \frac{\rule{1cm}{0.4pt}}{\rule{1cm}{0.4pt}}$$

Directions: Use proportions to solve each problem. Include the units in your answers.

A. A store has 9 shirts for every 3 jackets. How many shirts are there if the store has a total of 18 jackets?	**B.** A garden has 1 short pea plant for every 4 tall plants. If there are 20 short plants, how many tall plants are there?	**C.** The original iPod had 5 gigabytes of memory and held 1,000 songs. How many songs fit on a 20 gigabyte iPod?
D. Each room in a building has 2 doors and 8 windows. How many windows are there in all if there are 16 doors?	**E.** There are 4 short plants for every 2 tall ones. How many short plants are there if there are 100 tall ones?	**F.** How many days are there in 4 weeks? (You need to know three out of four numbers in order to solve a proportion, but this problem has only one known number given.)
G. How many weeks are there in 35 days?	**H.** Sally got 23 correct problems on a quiz with 25 total questions. If the quiz were to have 100 total questions, how many would she have gotten correct?	**I.** On another quiz, a student got 3 questions correct out of 4 total questions. If the quiz were to have 100 total questions, how many would the student have gotten correct?

Lesson 4: Setting Up and Solving Proportions

Write the Magic Formula here.

___ = ___

Directions: Use proportions to solve each problem. Include the units in your answers.

A.	B.	C.
Sally can read 2 pages in 6 minutes. How many minutes have passed by if she read 12 pages?	Tara can read 15 pages in 40 minutes. If she read 3 pages so far, how many minutes have passed by?	A store sells 4 red backpacks for every 10 green ones. If they sold 20 green backpacks, how many red backpacks were sold?
D.	E.	F.
A typical middle school student is 5 feet tall. Expressed in terms of inches, how tall is a typical middle school student?	How many inches tall is a 10-foot tree?	A car took 2 hours to travel 60 miles. At this rate, how far will it go in 6 hours?
G.	H.	I.
A jet can travel from California to Hawaii, a distance of 2,500 miles, in just 5 hours. How far can it travel in an hour?	How many hours are there in 3 days?	How many minutes are there in 5 hours?

Name_____

Lesson 5: Setting Up and Solving Proportions

Directions: Use proportions to solve each problem. Problem F and Problem H require unit conversions.

A. A school bus with a seating capacity of 60 students costs $310 to rent. How much would it cost to take 240 students on a field trip?	B. 20 pounds of potatoes costs $4. Laura spent $2. How many pounds of potatoes did she buy?	C. Gas costs $3 a gallon. A sport utility vehicle has a fuel tank capacity of 24 gallons. How much does it cost to fill up?
D. At $3 a gallon, it costs $36 to fill up a compact car's fuel tank. What is the fuel tank's capacity?	E. A water faucet is flowing at a rate of 24 gallons every 16 minutes. How long will it take 6 gallons to flow?	F. Water spills over Niagara Falls at a rate of 150,000 gallons per second. After a minute, how much water has gone over the falls?
G. Sound travels at 750 miles per hour. How far will sound travel in 3 hours?	H. During launch, the Space Shuttle traveled 300 miles per minute. At that rate, how far would it go in an hour?	I. A student got 37 questions correct out of 50 total questions. If the quiz were to have 100 questions, how many would the student get correct?

Making Sense of Proportions | © MathFluency.com | **Teachers: Log in for demo videos.** 15

Lesson 6: Setting Up and Solving Proportions

Directions: Use proportions to solve each problem. Note: Most of the numbers are in word form.

A. There are twenty girls in a class. If there are four boys for every five girls, how many boys are there?	**B.** There are four dogs for every three cats in a pet store. If there are twenty-four cats, how many dogs are there?	**C.** It costs $445 a month to lease the car of your dreams. Over the course of two years, how much have you paid to the car dealership?
D. The car of your dreams takes you on 159-mile trip in three hours. On the average, how far did you go in one hour?	**E.** A plane travels five kilometers in three minutes. How far will it travel in thirty minutes?	**F.** A student reads nine pages in eight minutes. At this rate, how long will it take to read a seventy-two-page chapter book?
G. Another student reads eight pages in six minutes. Twenty-four minutes have elapsed. How much has he read?	**H.** How many hours are there in four days?	**I.** A baby slept for six hours. How many minutes is that?

Name_____

Lesson 7: Setting Up and Solving Proportions – Speed Problems

Directions: Use proportions to solve each problem. Make sure your answers include the correct units.

A. A car travels 180 miles in three hours. How far will it go *per hour?*	B. A plane travels 640 miles in two hours. How far will it go *per hour?*	C. A runner runs four hundred meters in eighty seconds. How far will he run *per second?*
D. A car travels four hundred miles in eight hours. Find the speed. (How far will it go per hour?)	E. A plane travels four hundred miles in two hours. Find the speed. (How far will it go per hour?)	F. A runner runs eight hundred meters in one hundred seconds. Find the speed. (How far will he run per second?)
G. A snail crawls twenty-four inches in eight minutes. Find its speed.	H. A horse runs thirty-six miles in three hours. Find its speed.	I. A baseball is thrown ninety feet in three seconds. Find its speed.

Lesson 8: Deriving the Speed Formula from a Proportion

Part 1: Follow along with your instructor to derive the speed formula.

A.
A car travels 180 miles in three hours. How far will it go *per hour?*

_____ = _____

speed = _____ = _____ = _____

Part 2: Follow along with your instructor. Find the speed using the formula $s = \frac{d}{t}$.

B. Find the speed of a car traveling 130 miles in two hours.	C. Find the speed of a plane that travels 1,000 miles in four hours.	D. Find the speed of a runner running 26 miles in four hours.
E. Find the speed of a bird flying 1,800 miles in 6 days.	F. Sound can travel 1,500 miles in two hours. What is the speed of sound?	G. A train travels to a town 480 miles away in eight hours. What is its speed?
H. A train travels to a town 480 miles away in six hours. What is its speed?	I. A train travels to a town 480 miles away in just four hours. What is its speed?	J. A train travels to a town 480 miles away in just two hours. What is its speed?

Name_____

Lesson 9: Graphing a Proportional Relationship: Distance vs. Time

Directions: Follow along with your instructor. Use proportions to solve each problem. Then, graph your results.

A. A car travels 20 miles per hour. How far does it go in two hours?	B. How far does it go in three hours?	C. How far does it go in four hours?	D. How far does it go in five hours?

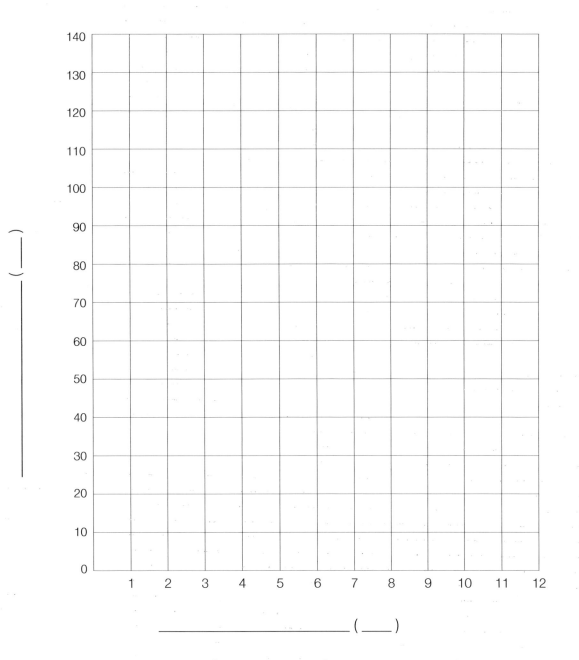

_____ (____)

Name_____

Lesson 10: Graphing Distance vs. Time

Directions: Use proportions to find the speed at each interval in the graph below. Label each segment with the speed.

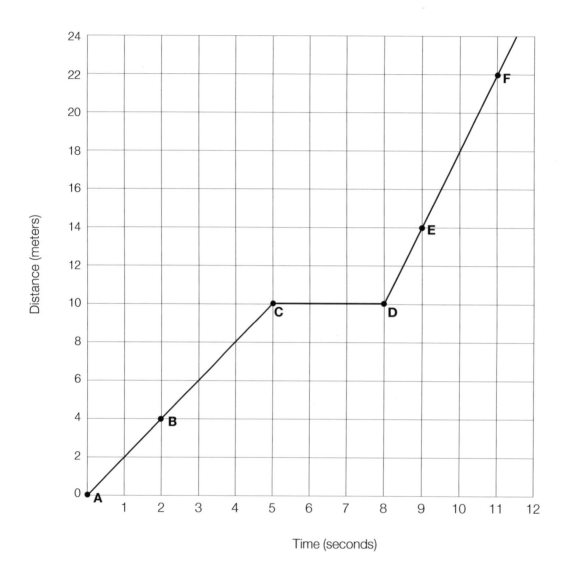

1. $\overline{AB}$	2. $\overline{BC}$	3. $\overline{AC}$	4. $\overline{CD}$
5. $\overline{DE}$	6. $\overline{EF}$	7. $\overline{DF}$	

Lesson 11: Graphing Distance vs. Time

Directions: Use proportions to solve each problem. Then, graph your results.

A. A car travels 10 miles per hour. How far does it go in two hours?	B. How far does it go in three hours?	C. How far does it go in four hours?	D. How far does it go in five hours?

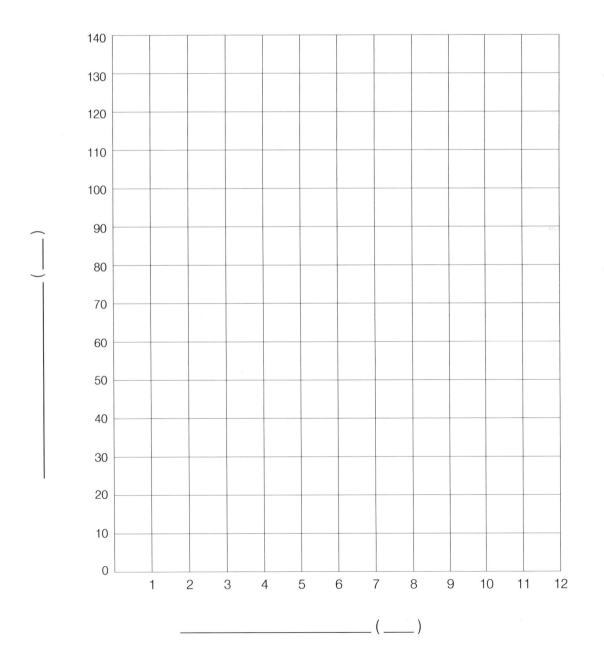

Name_____

Lesson 12: Graphing Distance vs. Time

Directions: Use proportions to find the speed at each interval in the graph below. Label each segment with the speed.

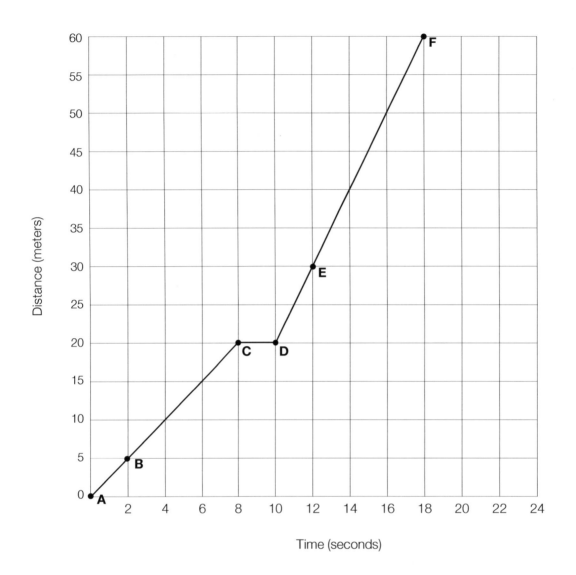

1. $\overline{AB}$	2. $\overline{BC}$	3. $\overline{AC}$	4. $\overline{CD}$
5. $\overline{DE}$	6. $\overline{EF}$	7. $\overline{DF}$	

Making Sense of Proportions | © MathFluency.com | **Teachers: Log in for demo videos.**

Name_____

Lesson 13: Calculating Distance with a Proportion in Disguise

Part 1: Simplify, then multiply.

A.	B.	C.	D.
$9 \times \dfrac{1}{9}$	$8 \times \dfrac{3}{8}$	$7 \times \dfrac{4}{7}$	$9 \times \dfrac{n}{9}$

Part 2: Follow along with your instructor to derive the formula for calculating the distance traveled.

Step 1 $\qquad \dfrac{mi}{hr} = \dfrac{mi}{hr}$

Step 2

Step 3

Step 4

The formula _____ = _____ · _____ is just a _____ _____ _____ .

Part 3: Solve each problem using the formula d = r · t. Hint: Take care of the numbers first, then take care of the units.

A. How far does a car traveling 40 miles per hour go in 6 hours?	B. After 3 hours, how far will a balloon float traveling 15 km/h?	C. A hurricane travels at 200 miles per day. How far will it go in 7 days?
D. A jet travels at 500 mph. How far will it go in eight hours?	E. Sound travels at 750 mph. How far will it go in three hours?	F. A sloth travels at 1.2 mph. How far will it go in 3 hours?

Lesson 14: Calculating Distance

Directions: Solve using the formula d = r · t. Include the units in your calculations and in your answers.

A. How far will a car go traveling 60 mph for three hours?	B. How far will a plane travel going 320 mph for two hours?	C. A runner runs at a rate of 5 meters per second. How far will he go in 80 seconds?
D. A car traveling 50 mph goes on an eight hour trip. How far did it go?	E. How far does a plane go at a speed of 200 mph for two hours?	F. A runner runs at a rate of 8 m/s for 100 seconds. How far will she travel?
G. A snail's speed is 3 in/min. What distance is covered in eight minutes?	H. A horse running at a rate of 12 kph runs for 3 hours. How far does it go?	I. A baseball travels at a rate of 30 feet per second for 3 seconds. How far does it go?

Name_____

Lesson 15: Graphing Distance vs. Time (Same Starting Point, Different Speeds)

Directions: Follow along with your instructor. Solve each problem using the formula d = rt. Graph your results.

A. At 5 mph, how far will a bicyclist go in four hours?	B. At 10 mph, how far will a bicyclist go in four hours?	C. At 15 mph, how far will a bicyclist go in four hours?

_____ - axis

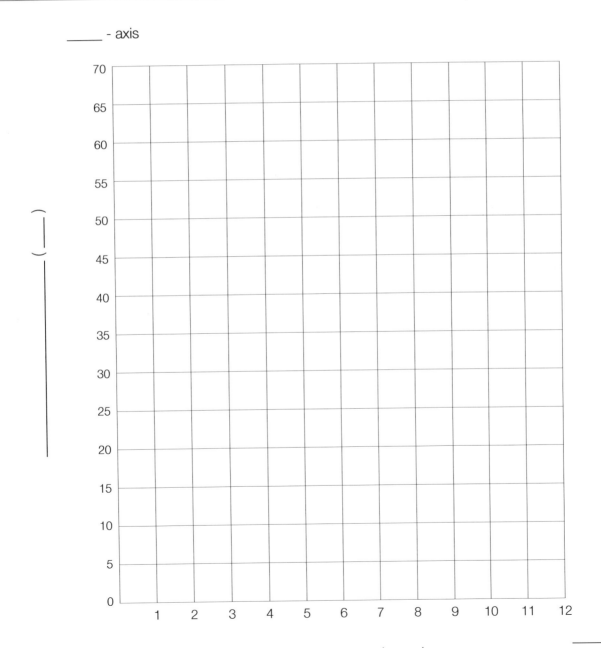

_____ - axis

_____ (_____)

Name_____

Lesson 16: Graphing Distance vs. Time (Same Speed, Different Starting Points)

Directions: Follow along with your instructor to solve each problem and to graph your results.

A.	B.	C.
At 5 mph, how far will a bicyclist go in four hours? Use d = rt.	A second bicyclist is going 5 mph as well, but she has a 10-mile head start. Without doing any calculations in this box, graph the equation. Follow along with your instructor.	A third bicyclist is going 5 mph as well, but he has a 15-mile head start. Without doing any calculations in this box, graph the equation. Follow along with your instructor.

_____ - axis

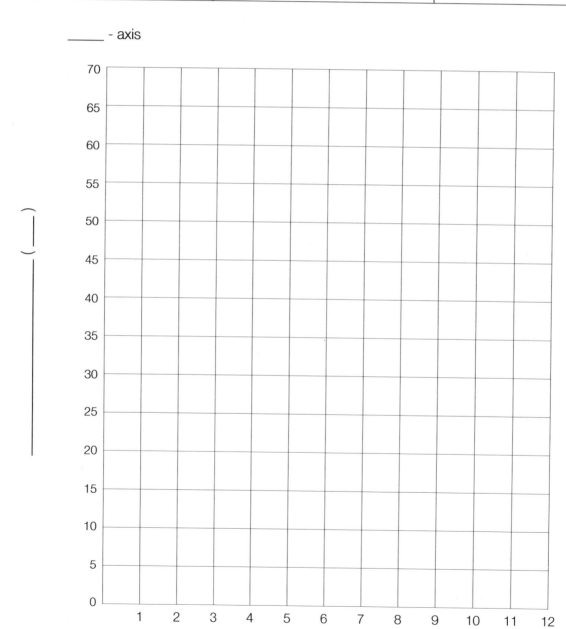

_____ - axis

_____ (____)

Name_____

Lesson 17: Calculating Distance with Changes in Units

Part 1: Write the correct relationship (expressed as a fraction) for each pair of units.

seconds & minutes	minutes & hours	hours & days	days & weeks	days & years

Part 2: Solve using the formula d = rt. Make sure your calculations and answers include the correct units.

A. How far will a car go traveling 60 mph for three days without stopping?	**B.** How far will a plane travel going eight miles per minute for two hours?
C. A snail travels at a rate of 3 in/min. What distance is covered in four hours?	**D.** How far would a plane go at a speed of 200 mph for two days?
E. A runner runs at a rate of 5 meters per second. How far will he travel in two hours? Careful! Multiple conversions and hanging zeroes.	**F.** At 5 m/s, how far will he go in three hours? Careful! Multiple conversions and hanging zeroes.

Lesson 18: Calculating Distance with Changes in Units

Part 1: Write the correct relationship (expressed as a fraction) for each pair of units.

seconds & minutes	minutes & hours	hours & days	days & weeks	days & years

Part 2: Solve using the formula d = rt. Make sure your calculations and answers include the correct units.

A. How far will a plane go traveling 90 mph for three days without stopping?	B. How far will a plane travel going ten miles per minute for two hours?
C. A snail travels at a rate of 2 in/min. What distance is covered in five hours?	D. How far would a plane go at a speed of 100 mph for three days?
E. A runner runs at a rate of 6 meters per second. How far will he travel in two hours? Careful! Multiple conversions and hanging zeroes.	F. A runner runs at a rate of 6 m/s. How far will he go in one hour? Careful! Multiple conversions and hanging zeroes.

Lesson 19: Calculating Distance with Changes in Units

Part 1: Write the correct relationship (expressed as a fraction) for each pair of units.

seconds & minutes	minutes & hours	hours & days	days & weeks	days & years

Part 2: Solve using the formula d = rt. Make sure your calculations and answers include the correct units.

A. A car on the freeway travels 90 feet per second. How far does it go in 5 seconds?	B. How far will it go in 5 minutes?
C. The Space Shuttle travels at a rate of 18,000 mph. How far does it go in three days?	D. At three meters per second, what distance is covered by an athlete running for two hours? Careful! Multiple conversions and hanging zeroes.
E. A bird flies at a rate of 12 meters per second. How far will it go in 4 hours? Careful! Multiple conversions and hanging zeroes.	F. A bird flies at a rate of 4 meters per second. How far will it go in 8 hours? Careful! Multiple conversions and hanging zeroes.

Lesson 20: Calculating Distance with Changes in Units

Part 1: Write the correct relationship (expressed as a fraction) for each pair of units.

seconds & minutes	minutes & hours	hours & days	days & weeks	months & years

Part 2: Solve using the formula d = rt. Make sure your calculations and answers include the correct units.

A. A tree grows three inches per month. How much taller will it be in 4 years?	B. A ship travels at a rate of 30 mph. How far will it go on a six day cruise?
C. An arrow traveling 200 feet per second hits its target in three seconds. How far away is the target?	D. A glacier travels 30 meters per day. How far does it travel in 3 weeks?
E. At the equator, the earth rotates 25,000 miles in one day. How far does it rotate in two weeks? Careful! Hanging zeroes.	F. At the equator, the earth rotates 25,000 miles in one day. How far does it rotate in the month of April? Careful! Hanging zeroes.

Answer Keys and Correcting Student Work

The answer keys in this section are fully annotated. They show not only the correct answer, but how to get there. This makes is easier to troubleshoot student errors so they can correct them.

Provide immediate feedback so that students know how they are doing. Take a look at the sample work below.

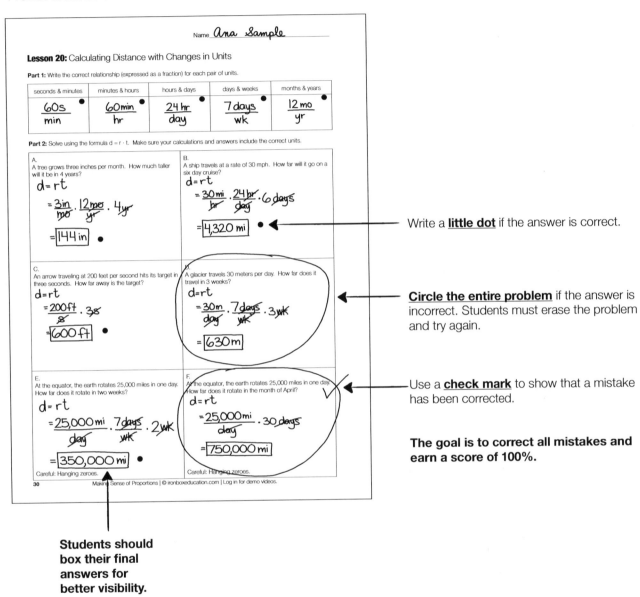

Write a **little dot** if the answer is correct.

Circle the entire problem if the answer is incorrect. Students must erase the problem and try again.

Use a **check mark** to show that a mistake has been corrected.

The goal is to correct all mistakes and earn a score of 100%.

Students should box their final answers for better visibility.

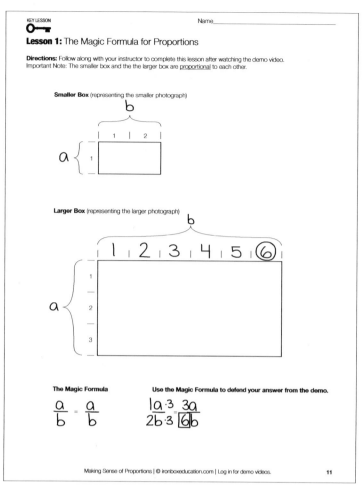

KEY LESSON

Name_____

Lesson 1: The Magic Formula for Proportions

Directions: Follow along with your instructor to complete this lesson after watching the demo video.
Important Note: The smaller box and the the larger box are proportional to each other.

Smaller Box (representing the smaller photograph)

Larger Box (representing the larger photograph)

The Magic Formula

$$\frac{a}{b} = \frac{a}{b}$$

Use the Magic Formula to defend your answer from the demo.

$$\frac{1a \cdot 3}{2b \cdot 3} = \frac{3a}{6b}$$

Making Sense of Proportions | © ironboxeducation.com | Log in for demo videos.   11

Key Points from Demo Video – Lesson 1
The Magic Formula for Proportions

Lesson 1 starts off with a demo video that explains visually why proportions matter. The video shows a photograph being stretched disproportionately, which causes the photo to become distorted (either too tall or too wide).

To prevent distortion, the photograph must be stretched proportionately. If you make it twice as tall, you must also make it twice as wide.

A proportion uses four values to describe a relationship. If you're given three of the values, you can use an equivalent fraction to figure out the missing value.

The reason students struggle with proportions is that they simply don't know how to set it up properly. Without a system, students have a 50% chance of setting up the proportion incorrectly. Those are not good odds, and it leads to frustration.

The Magic Formula is the simple way to properly set up and solve any proportion. The Magic Formula is:

$$\frac{a}{b} = \frac{a}{b}$$

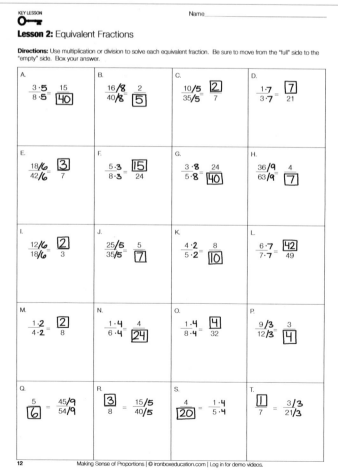

KEY LESSON

Name_____

Lesson 2: Equivalent Fractions

Directions: Use multiplication or division to solve each equivalent fraction. Be sure to move from the "full" side to the "empty" side. Box your answer.

A. $\frac{3 \cdot 5}{8 \cdot 5} = \frac{15}{\boxed{40}}$

B. $\frac{16/8}{40/8} = \frac{2}{\boxed{5}}$

C. $\frac{10/5}{35/5} = \frac{\boxed{2}}{7}$

D. $\frac{1 \cdot 7}{3 \cdot 7} = \frac{\boxed{7}}{21}$

E. $\frac{18/6}{42/6} = \frac{\boxed{3}}{7}$

F. $\frac{5 \cdot 3}{8 \cdot 3} = \frac{\boxed{15}}{24}$

G. $\frac{3 \cdot 8}{5 \cdot 8} = \frac{24}{\boxed{40}}$

H. $\frac{36/9}{63/9} = \frac{4}{\boxed{7}}$

I. $\frac{12/6}{18/6} = \frac{\boxed{2}}{3}$

J. $\frac{25/5}{35/5} = \frac{5}{\boxed{7}}$

K. $\frac{4 \cdot 2}{5 \cdot 2} = \frac{8}{\boxed{10}}$

L. $\frac{6 \cdot 7}{7 \cdot 7} = \frac{\boxed{42}}{49}$

M. $\frac{1 \cdot 2}{4 \cdot 2} = \frac{\boxed{2}}{8}$

N. $\frac{1 \cdot 4}{6 \cdot 4} = \frac{4}{\boxed{24}}$

O. $\frac{1 \cdot 4}{8 \cdot 4} = \frac{\boxed{4}}{32}$

P. $\frac{9/3}{12/3} = \frac{3}{\boxed{4}}$

Q. $\frac{5}{\boxed{6}} = \frac{45/9}{54/9}$

R. $\frac{\boxed{3}}{8} = \frac{15/5}{40/5}$

S. $\frac{4}{\boxed{20}} = \frac{1 \cdot 4}{5 \cdot 4}$

T. $\frac{\boxed{1}}{7} = \frac{3/3}{21/3}$

12   Making Sense of Proportions | © ironboxeducation.com | Log in for demo videos.

Key Points from Demo Video – Lesson 2
Equivalent Fractions

Once you set up a proportion properly using the Magic Formula, it just becomes a matter of solving an equivalent fraction. This means that students must be fluent working with equivalent fractions.

In this lesson, students use multiplication or division to solve each equivalent fraction. Keep the following in mind:

- Students should go from the "full" side (the complete fraction) to the "empty" side (the fraction with a missing value).
- Sometimes, the empty side is on the right of the equal sign. Other times, it will be on the left.
- Sometimes, the missing value will be in the numerator. Other times, the missing value will be in the denominator.
- Some problems require multiplication to find the missing value. Other times, division will be used.

This lesson uses these various combinations so that students are prepared to deal with any type of equivalent fraction that they encounter.

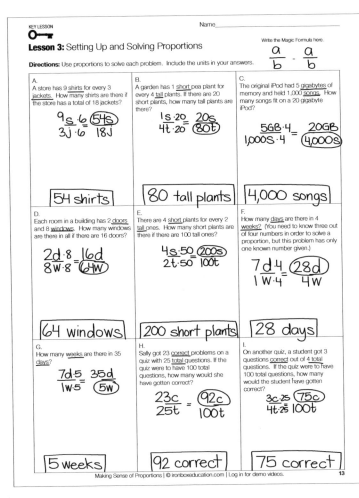

Key Points from Demo Video – Lesson 3
Setting Up and Solving Proportions

In Lesson 3, students solve proportion word problems easily using the Magic Formula. Students start off by writing the Magic Formula in the space provided to the right of the directions. The Magic Formula is:

$$\frac{a}{b} = \frac{a}{b}$$

The first problem has no a's and b's. Instead, there are shirts and jackets. The proportion is:

$$\frac{s}{j} = \frac{s}{j}$$

Students should leave enough space so that they have room to show their work.

As shown in the answer key and in the demo video, the answer to Box A is 54 shirts. Remember to include the units in answer. An answer of "54" would be insufficient. The correct answer is "54 shirts," which you will notice answers the question, "How many shirts are there?"

Students also learn what to do when the problem doesn't give them the three out of four values that they need to solve a proportion (Box F).

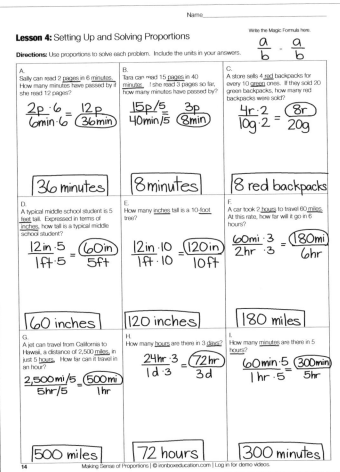

Key Points from Demo Video – Lesson 4
Setting Up and Solving Proportions

Lesson 4 builds upon Lesson 3, and students continue setting up and solving proportions using the Magic Formula.

Remember that when solving a proportion, you need to know three of the four values in order to figure out the missing value.

Problems D, E, H, and I appear not give students the three values that they need (only one value is given). Students must use their prior knowledge about key relationships to figure out the two missing values. The relationships in this lesson are:

- 12 inches in 1 foot
- 24 hours in 1 day
- 60 minutes in 1 hour

Students should use hanging zeroes in Box G to solve 2500 ÷ 5.

Remember to have students box their final answers as shown in the answer key for better visibility.

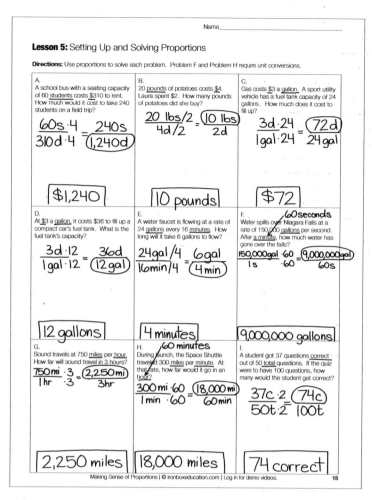

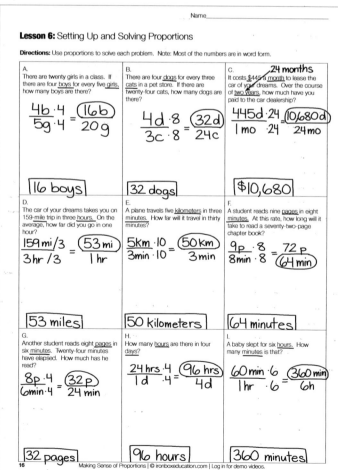

Key Points from Demo Video – Lesson 5
Setting Up and Solving Proportions

In Lesson 5, students continue setting up and solving proportions. This set of problems includes a couple of tricky problems that use conversions and hanging zeroes.

Box F says that water spills over Niagara Falls at a rate of 150,000 gallons per <u>second</u>. However, it asks how much water has gone over the falls in one <u>minute</u>.

Minutes and seconds are not the same unit of time. Convert one minute to 60 seconds so that the proportion can be set up properly as:

$$\frac{gal}{s} = \frac{gal}{s}$$

The Niagara Falls question also involves hanging zeroes to multiply 150,000 x 60.

Box H says that the Space Shuttle travels 300 miles per <u>minute.</u> However, it asks how far it would go in an <u>hour.</u> Convert one hour to 60 minutes. This problem also includes hanging zeroes to calculate 300 x 60.

Key Points from Demo Video – Lesson 6
Setting Up and Solving Proportions

In Lesson 6, students need to think a little harder, as most of the numbers are now spelled out in word form. For example, the numbers 20, 4, and 5 are spelled out as twenty, four, and five

Also, this lesson includes a couple more tricky problems that are worded differently and involve conversions.

Box A, for example, is worded differently from previous problems. In previous problems, if students set up the proportion by writing down the information as it's written in the word problem, the "empty" side of the proportion ends up on the right, which is a format that they are accustomed to seeing.

In Box A, however, they will end up with the "empty" side of the proportion on the left. Students can switch the left side and the right side of the equation to make it easier to solve.

Box C requires converting "two years" into "24 months."

Box H requires knowing that there are 24 hours in one day.

Making Sense of Proportions | © MathFluency.com | **Teachers: Log in for demo videos.**

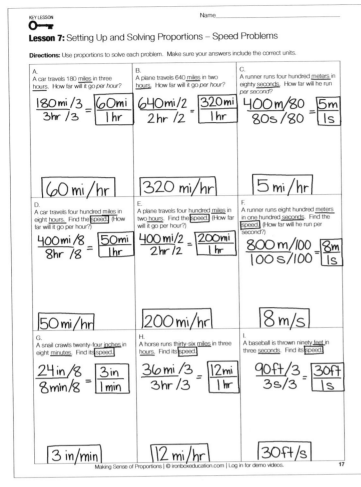

KEY LESSON

Lesson 7: Setting Up and Solving Proportions – Speed Problems

Name_____

Directions: Use proportions to solve each problem. Make sure your answers include the correct units.

A.
A car travels 180 miles in three hours. How far will it go *per hour?*

$$\frac{180 \text{ mi}/3}{3 \text{ hr}/3} = \boxed{\frac{60 \text{ mi}}{1 \text{ hr}}}$$

$$\boxed{60 \text{ mi/hr}}$$

B.
A plane travels 640 miles in two hours. How far will it go *per hour?*

$$\frac{640 \text{ mi}/2}{2 \text{ hr}/2} = \boxed{\frac{320 \text{ mi}}{1 \text{ hr}}}$$

$$\boxed{320 \text{ mi/hr}}$$

C.
A runner runs four hundred meters in eighty seconds. How far will he run per second?

$$\frac{400 \text{ m}/80}{80 \text{ s}/80} = \boxed{\frac{5 \text{ m}}{1 \text{ s}}}$$

$$\boxed{5 \text{ mi/hr}}$$

D.
A car travels four hundred miles in eight hours. Find the speed. (How far will it go per hour?)

$$\frac{400 \text{ mi}/8}{8 \text{ hr}/8} = \boxed{\frac{50 \text{ mi}}{1 \text{ hr}}}$$

$$\boxed{50 \text{ mi/hr}}$$

E.
A plane travels four hundred miles in two hours. Find the speed. (How far will it go per hour?)

$$\frac{400 \text{ mi}/2}{2 \text{ hr}/2} = \boxed{\frac{200 \text{ mi}}{1 \text{ hr}}}$$

$$\boxed{200 \text{ mi/hr}}$$

F.
A runner runs eight hundred meters in one hundred seconds. Find the speed. (How far will he run per second?)

$$\frac{800 \text{ m}/100}{100 \text{ s}/100} = \boxed{\frac{8 \text{ m}}{1 \text{ s}}}$$

$$\boxed{8 \text{ m/s}}$$

G.
A snail crawls twenty-four inches in eight minutes. Find its speed.

$$\frac{24 \text{ in}/8}{8 \text{ min}/8} = \boxed{\frac{3 \text{ in}}{1 \text{ min}}}$$

$$\boxed{3 \text{ in/min}}$$

H.
A horse runs thirty-six miles in three hours. Find its speed.

$$\frac{36 \text{ mi}/3}{3 \text{ hr}/3} = \boxed{\frac{12 \text{ mi}}{1 \text{ hr}}}$$

$$\boxed{12 \text{ mi/hr}}$$

I.
A baseball is thrown ninety feet in three seconds. Find its speed.

$$\frac{90 \text{ ft}/3}{3 \text{ s}/3} = \boxed{\frac{30 \text{ ft}}{1 \text{ s}}}$$

$$\boxed{30 \text{ ft/s}}$$

Making Sense of Proportions | © ironboxeducation.com | Log in for demo videos. 17

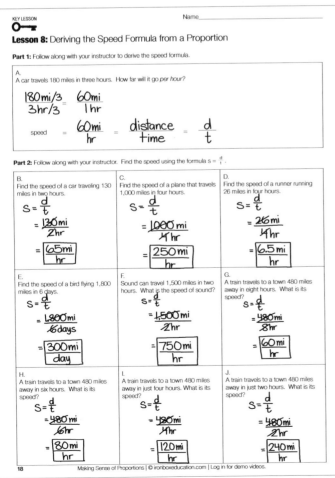

KEY LESSON

Lesson 8: Deriving the Speed Formula from a Proportion

Name_____

Part 1: Follow along with your instructor to derive the speed formula.

A.
A car travels 180 miles in three hours. How far will it go *per hour?*

$$\frac{180 \text{ mi}/3}{3 \text{ hr}/3} = \frac{60 \text{ mi}}{1 \text{ hr}}$$

$$\text{speed} = \frac{60 \text{ mi}}{\text{hr}} = \frac{\text{distance}}{\text{time}} = \frac{d}{t}$$

Part 2: Follow along with your instructor. Find the speed using the formula $s = \frac{d}{t}$.

B.
Find the speed of a car traveling 130 miles in two hours.

$$s = \frac{d}{t}$$
$$= \frac{130 \text{ mi}}{2 \text{ hr}}$$
$$= \boxed{\frac{65 \text{ mi}}{\text{hr}}}$$

C.
Find the speed of a plane that travels 1,000 miles in four hours.

$$s = \frac{d}{t}$$
$$= \frac{1000 \text{ mi}}{4 \text{ hr}}$$
$$= \boxed{\frac{250 \text{ mi}}{\text{hr}}}$$

D.
Find the speed of a runner running 26 miles in four hours.

$$s = \frac{d}{t}$$
$$= \frac{26 \text{ mi}}{4 \text{ hr}}$$
$$= \boxed{\frac{6.5 \text{ mi}}{\text{hr}}}$$

E.
Find the speed of a bird flying 1,800 miles in 6 days.

$$s = \frac{d}{t}$$
$$= \frac{1800 \text{ mi}}{6 \text{ days}}$$
$$= \boxed{\frac{300 \text{ mi}}{\text{day}}}$$

F.
Sound can travel 1,500 miles in two hours. What is the speed of sound?

$$s = \frac{d}{t}$$
$$= \frac{1500 \text{ mi}}{2 \text{ hr}}$$
$$= \boxed{\frac{750 \text{ mi}}{\text{hr}}}$$

G.
A train travels to a town 480 miles away in eight hours. What is its speed?

$$s = \frac{d}{t}$$
$$= \frac{480 \text{ mi}}{8 \text{ hr}}$$
$$= \boxed{\frac{60 \text{ mi}}{\text{hr}}}$$

H.
A train travels to a town 480 miles away in six hours. What is its speed?

$$s = \frac{d}{t}$$
$$= \frac{480 \text{ mi}}{6 \text{ hr}}$$
$$= \boxed{\frac{80 \text{ mi}}{\text{hr}}}$$

I.
A train travels to a town 480 miles away in just four hours. What is its speed?

$$s = \frac{d}{t}$$
$$= \frac{480 \text{ mi}}{4 \text{ hr}}$$
$$= \boxed{\frac{120 \text{ mi}}{\text{hr}}}$$

J.
A train travels to a town 480 miles away in just two hours. What is its speed?

$$s = \frac{d}{t}$$
$$= \frac{480 \text{ mi}}{2 \text{ hr}}$$
$$= \boxed{\frac{240 \text{ mi}}{\text{hr}}}$$

18   Making Sense of Proportions | © ironboxeducation.com | Log in for demo videos.

Key Points from Demo Video – Lesson 7
Setting Up and Solving Proportions: Speed Problems

Lesson 7 uses proportions to introduce the concept of speed. This is an example of how proportions run deep into the heart of math since speed involves a proportional relationship between distance in time.

The proportional relationship in Box A is:

$$\frac{\text{mi}}{\text{hr}} = \frac{\text{mi}}{\text{hr}}$$

The question asks not just how far the car will travel, but how far will it travel <u>per hour.</u> "Per hour" means "per 1 hour," so students should remember that the number "1" is part of the proportional relationship.

Since this is a speed problem that asks not just how how far the car will go, but rather, how far the car will go <u>per hour</u>, students must box the entire fraction on the right side, which shows the speed. As shown in the answer key, the car's speed in Box A is "60 miles per 1 hour," or simply, "60 miles per hour."

An answer of "60 miles" would be insufficient. "60 miles" answers the distance question, "How far?" However, the speed question is asking, "How far <u>per hour</u>?"

Key Points from Demo Video – Lesson 8
Deriving the Speed Formula from a Proportion

In Lesson 8, students follow along with their instructor to derive the speed formula. This will help them see that hidden within the Magic Formula for Proportions is the speed formula.

The initial setup in Box A is:

$$\frac{\text{mi}}{\text{hr}} = \frac{\text{mi}}{\text{hr}}$$

This helps students figure out the speed:

$$\text{speed} = \frac{60 \text{ mi}}{\text{hr}}$$

From here, students see that:

$$\text{speed} = \frac{60 \text{ mi}}{\text{hr}} = \frac{\text{distance}}{\text{time}} = \frac{d}{t}$$

For the remaining problems, students use the formula $s = d/t$ to figure out the speed.

In Part 2, students should use slashes to show that fractions are being simplified (Box B shows slashes through 130 and 2, which are both being divided by the GCF of 2. Also, the correct units must be used. The full and correct answer in Box B is 65 mi/hr.

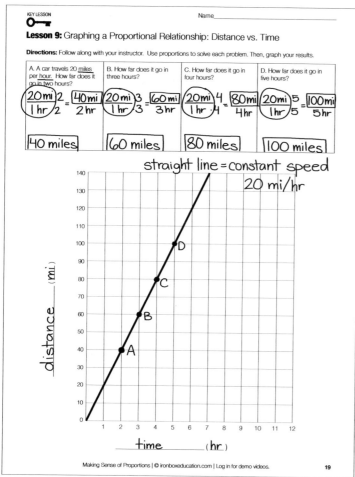

KEY LESSON
O━

Name_____

Lesson 9: Graphing a Proportional Relationship: Distance vs. Time

Directions: Follow along with your instructor. Use proportions to solve each problem. Then, graph your results.

A. A car travels 20 miles per hour. How far does it go in two hours?	B. How far does it go in three hours?	C. How far does it go in four hours?	D. How far does it go in five hours?
$\frac{20mi}{1hr} \cdot \frac{2}{2} = \frac{40mi}{2hr}$	$\frac{20mi}{1hr} \cdot \frac{3}{3} = \frac{60mi}{3hr}$	$\frac{20mi}{1hr} \cdot \frac{4}{4} = \frac{80mi}{4hr}$	$\frac{20mi}{1hr} \cdot \frac{5}{5} = \frac{100mi}{5hr}$
40 miles	60 miles	80 miles	100 miles

straight line = constant speed

20 mi/hr

distance ____ (mi)

time ____ (hr)

Making Sense of Proportions | © ironboxeducation.com | Log in for demo videos.   19

KEY LESSON
O━

Name_____

Lesson 10: Graphing Distance vs. Time

Directions: Use proportions to find the speed at each interval in the graph below. Label each segment with the speed.

Distance (meters)

4 m/s
4 m/s
0 m/s
flat line = not moving
4 m/s
2 m/s
2 m/s
2 m/s

Time (seconds)

1. $\overline{AB}$	2. $\overline{BC}$	3. $\overline{AC}$	4. $\overline{CD}$
$\frac{4m/2}{2s/2} = \frac{2m}{1s}$	$\frac{6m/3}{3s/3} = \frac{2m}{1s}$	$\frac{10m/5}{5s/5} = \frac{2m}{1s}$	$\frac{0m/3}{3s/3} = \frac{0m}{1s}$
2 m/s	2 m/s	2 m/s	0 m/s

5. $\overline{DE}$	6. $\overline{EF}$	7. $\overline{DF}$	
$\frac{4m}{1s}$	$\frac{8m/2}{2s/2} = \frac{4m}{1s}$	$\frac{12m/3}{3s/3} = \frac{4m}{1s}$	
4 m/s	4 m/s	4 m/s	

20   Making Sense of Proportions | © ironboxeducation.com | Log in for demo videos.

Key Points from Demo Video – Lesson 9

Graphing a Proportional Relationship: Distance vs. Time

In Lesson 9, students learn how to graph a proportional relationship, and they see what constant speed looks like on a graph.

This lesson is another prime example of how proportions run deep into the heart of algebra.

In Boxes A-D, a car is traveling at a rate of 20 miles per hour. Students use proportions to find the distance traveled at two hours, three hours, four hours, and five hours.

Then, students graph this information on the graph with their instructor. Be sure to label the x-axis as "time (hr)," and label the y-axis as "distance (mi)."

Notice that since the car is moving at a constant speed of 20 miles per hour, it forms a straight line on the graph.

Key Points from Demo Video – Lesson 10

Graphing Distance vs. Time

The previous lesson graphed an object moving at a constant speed.

In Lesson 10, students graph an object that changes speed at different points in time. Students use proportions to determine the speed at each segment.

Box 1 shows the line segment $\overline{AB}$. The distance traveled from point A to Point B is 4 meters, and the elapsed time is 2 seconds. Students use a proportion to find that the speed of line segment $\overline{AB}$ is 2 m/s. Students label line segment $\overline{AB}$ on the graph with the speed of 2 m/s.

Continue on with the remaining line segments.

Notice that line segments $\overline{AB}$, $\overline{BC}$, and $\overline{AC}$ all have a speed of 2 m/s. You can tell that the speed is the same along these segments because they form a straight line.

Between point C and point D, the object is not moving (0 m/s). You can tell because the line is flat. Points D, E, and F form another straight line, and the speed along these segments is 4 m/s.

36   Making Sense of Proportions | © MathFluency.com | **Teachers: Log in for demo videos.**

Name_____

Lesson 11: Graphing Distance vs. Time

Directions: Use proportions to solve each problem. Then, graph your results.

A. A car travels 10 miles per hour. How far does it go in two hours?	B. How far does it go in three hours?	C. How far does it go in four hours?	D. How far does it go in five hours?
$\frac{10\,mi}{1\,hr} \cdot \frac{2}{2} = \frac{20\,mi}{2\,hr}$	$\frac{10\,mi}{1\,hr} \cdot \frac{3}{3} = \frac{30\,mi}{3\,hr}$	$\frac{10\,mi}{1\,hr} \cdot \frac{4}{4} = \frac{40\,mi}{4\,hr}$	$\frac{10\,mi}{1\,hr} \cdot \frac{5}{5} = \frac{50\,mi}{5\,hr}$
20 miles	30 miles	40 miles	50 miles

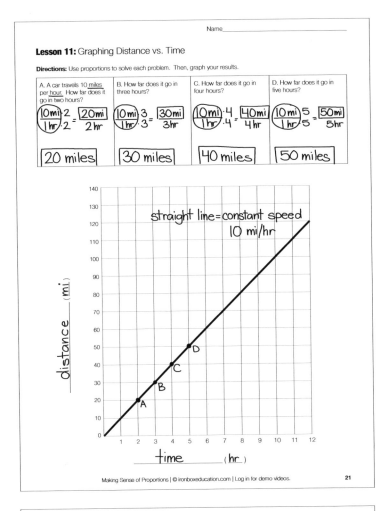

straight line = constant speed
10 mi/hr

distance (mi)

time (hr)

Making Sense of Proportions | © ironboxeducation.com | Log in for demo videos. 21

Key Points from Demo Video – Lesson 11
Graphing Distance vs. Time

In Lesson 11, students practice the graphing skills that they first learned in Lesson 9.

The car in this lesson is moving at a rate of 10 miles per hour instead of 20 miles per hour.

Since this is very similar to the graphing exercise from Lesson 9, the instructor should hand off more off the lesson to the students (for example, calling on students to explain what step comes next.

Once again, students should notice that since the car is traveling at a constant speed of 10 miles per hour, the graph will form a straight line.

Be sure to label the x-axis as "time (hr)" and the y-axis as "distance (mi)."

Name_____

Lesson 12: Graphing Distance vs. Time

Directions: Use proportions to find the speed at each interval in the graph below. Label each segment with the speed.

Distance (meters)

5 m/s, 5 m/s, 5 m/s, 0 m/s, 2.5 m/s, 2.5 m/s, 2.5 m/s
flat line = not moving

Time (seconds)

1. $\overline{AB}$	2. $\overline{BC}$	3. $\overline{AC}$	4. $\overline{CD}$
$\frac{5m/2}{2s/2} = \frac{2.5m}{1s}$	$\frac{15m/6}{6s/6} = \frac{2.5m}{1s}$	$\frac{20m/8}{8s/8} = \frac{2.5m}{1s}$	$\frac{0m/2}{2s/2} = \frac{0m}{1s}$
2.5 m/s	2.5 m/s	2.5 m/s	0 m/s

5. $\overline{DE}$	6. $\overline{EF}$	7. $\overline{DF}$	
$\frac{10m/2}{2s/2} = \frac{5m}{1s}$	$\frac{30m/6}{6s/6} = \frac{5m}{1s}$	$\frac{40m/8}{8s/8} = \frac{5m}{1s}$	
5 m/s	5 m/s	5 m/s	

22   Making Sense of Proportions | © ironboxeducation.com | Log in for demo videos.

Key Points from Demo Video – Lesson 12
Graphing Distance vs. Time

Lesson 12 is the sister lesson to Lesson 10, and students practice the graphing skills that they learned previously.

However, Lesson 12 has a couple of important differences, so be careful.

- The scale on the x-axis (time) uses increments of 2 instead of increments of 1.
- The scale on the y-axis (distance) uses increments of 5 instead of increments of 2.
- Lesson 12 includes decimals. For example, the speed along line segment $\overline{AB}$ is 2.5 m/s.

Again, key points from the graph are:

- A straight line indicates constant speed.
- A flat line indicates that the object is not moving.

Lesson 13: Calculating Distance with a Proportion in Disguise

Part 1: Simplify, then multiply.

A.	B.	C.	D.
$\not{8} \times \frac{1}{\not{8}} = 1$	$\not{8} \times \frac{3}{\not{8}} = 3$	$\not{7} \times \frac{4}{\not{7}} = 4$	$\not{8} \times \frac{n}{\not{8}} = n$

Part 2: Follow along with your instructor to derive the formula for calculating the distance traveled.

Step 1 $\not{hr} \cdot \frac{mi}{\not{hr}} = \frac{mi}{hr} \cdot hr$

Step 2 $mi = \frac{mi}{hr} \cdot hr$

Step 3 $distance = rate \cdot time$

Step 4 $d = r \cdot t$

The formula $\underline{d} = \underline{r} \cdot \underline{t}$ is just a $\underline{proportion \quad in \quad disguise}$

Part 3: Solve each problem using the formula d = r · t. Hint: Take care of the numbers first, then take care of the units.

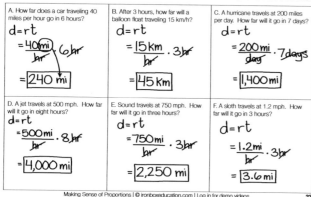

A. How far does a car traveling 40 miles per hour go in 6 hours?	B. After 3 hours, how far will a balloon float traveling 15 km/h?	C. A hurricane travels at 200 miles per day. How far will it go in 7 days?
$d = rt$ $= \frac{40\,mi}{\not{hr}} \cdot 6\,\not{hr}$ $= \boxed{240\ mi}$	$d = rt$ $= \frac{15\,km}{\not{hr}} \cdot 3\,\not{hr}$ $= \boxed{45\,km}$	$d = rt$ $= \frac{200\,mi}{\not{day}} \cdot 7\,\not{days}$ $= \boxed{1,400\,mi}$
D. A jet travels at 500 mph. How far will it go in eight hours?	E. Sound travels at 750 mph. How far will it go in three hours?	F. A sloth travels at 1.2 mph. How far will it go in 3 hours?
$d = rt$ $= \frac{500\,mi}{\not{hr}} \cdot 8\,\not{hr}$ $= \boxed{4,000\,mi}$	$d = rt$ $= \frac{750\,mi}{\not{hr}} \cdot 3\,\not{hr}$ $= \boxed{2,250\,mi}$	$d = rt$ $= \frac{1.2\,mi}{\not{hr}} \cdot 3\,\not{hr}$ $= \boxed{3.6\,mi}$

Name_____

Lesson 14: Calculating Distance

Directions: Solve using the formula d = r · t. Include the units in your calculations and in your answers.

A. How far will a car go traveling 60 mph for three hours?	B. How far will a plane travel going 320 mph for two hours?	C. A runner runs at a rate of 5 meters per second. How far will he go in 80 seconds?
$d = rt$ $= \frac{60\,mi}{\not{hr}} \cdot 3\,\not{hr}$ $= \boxed{180\,mi}$	$d = rt$ $= \frac{320\,mi}{\not{hr}} \cdot 2\,\not{hr}$ $= \boxed{640\,mi}$	$d = rt$ $= \frac{5\,m}{\not{s}} \cdot 80\,\not{s}$ $= \boxed{400\,m}$
D. A car traveling 50 mph goes on an eight hour trip. How far did it go?	E. How far does a plane go at a speed of 200 mph for two hours?	F. A runner runs at a rate of 8 m/s for 100 seconds. How far will she travel?
$d = rt$ $= \frac{50\,mi}{\not{hr}} \cdot 8\,\not{hr}$ $= \boxed{400\,mi}$	$d = rt$ $= \frac{200\,mi}{\not{hr}} \cdot 2\,\not{hr}$ $= \boxed{400\,mi}$	$d = rt$ $= \frac{8\,m}{\not{s}} \cdot 100\,\not{s}$ $= \boxed{800\,m}$
G. A snail's speed is 3 in/min. What distance is covered in eight minutes?	H. A horse running at a rate of 12 kph runs for 3 hours. How far does it go?	I. A baseball travels at a rate of 30 feet per second for 3 seconds. How far does it go?
$d = rt$ $= \frac{3\,in}{\not{min}} \cdot 8\,\not{min}$ $= \boxed{24\,in}$	$d = rt$ $= \frac{12\,km}{\not{hr}} \cdot 3\,\not{hr}$ $= \boxed{36\,km}$	$d = rt$ $= \frac{30\,ft}{\not{s}} \cdot 3\,\not{s}$ $= \boxed{90\,ft}$

Key Points from Demo Video – Lesson 13
Calculating Distance with a Proportion in Disguise

In this extremely important lesson, students learn that the well-known algebraic formula d = rt is really just a proportion in disguise. This is yet another prime example of how proportions run deep into the heart of algebra.

In Part 1, students practice simplifying fractions before multiplying. This will help them follow along with the logic in Part 2.

In Part 2, students follow along with their instructor to derive the formula for calculating the distance traveled.

Students start off in Step 1 with the familiar proportion mi/hr = mi/hr. The demo video shows how to derive the formula for calculating the distance traveled, which is d = r · t. This shows that the well-known formula d = r · t started off as a proportion and is really just a proportion in disguise.

Now that students know where the formula d = r · t came from and they know that it actually works, they will use it to solve distance problems in Part 3. Students must include the units in their calculations and in their final answers.

Key Points from Demo Video – Lesson 14
Calculating Distance

In Lesson 14, students use the formula d = r · t to solve proportion problems involving distance.

As in the previous lesson, students must include the units in their calculations and in their final answers.

Including the units is important because it helps students keep track of the meaning behind the numbers that they are working with.

For example, in Box A, if students only write "180" as their answer without any units, the "180" could mean any of the following:

- 180 miles (a distance)
- 180 miles per hour (a speed)
- 180 hours (a length of time)

All three of these measures mean different things, so the units do matter. The questions asks, "How far?" which is a distance question. Therefore, the only logical answer is 180 miles.

Notice in Box A that both the units "mi" and "hr" were included in the calculations. The units of "hr" cancel out, leaving "mi" as the only remaining unit.

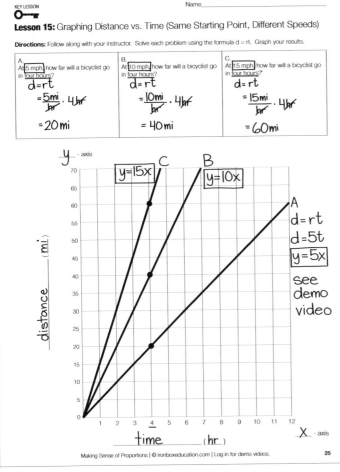

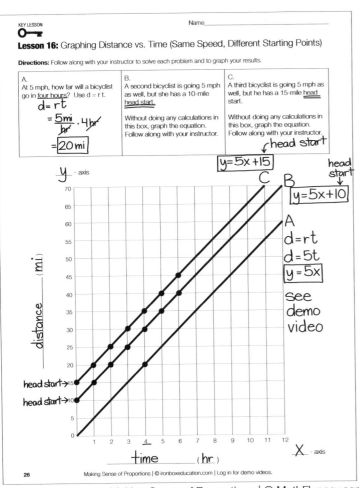

Key Points from Demo Video – Lesson 15
Graphing Distance vs. Time (Same Starting Point, Different Speeds)

In yet another important lesson, students continue graphing in Lesson 15. Here, students add the formula d = rt to their graphing repertoire.

The objects being graphed will all have the same starting points, but they are traveling at different speeds.

In Boxes A, B, and C, students calculate the distance traveled using the formula d = rt.

Students then graph this information. They label each line as lines A, B, and C. Bicyclist C is the fastest at 15 mph, and that's why its line is the steepest.

For line A, notice that the formula d = rt is written down. Remember that d = rt is a proportion in disguise (Lesson 13). The rate (or speed) for line A is 5 miles per hour, so **d = rt** is rewritten as **d = 5t.**

The distance (d) is on the y-axis, and the time (t) is on the x-axis. Therefore, **d = 5t** is rewritten as **y = 5x.** This shows that formulas such as y = 5x are also proportional relationships.

Key Points from Demo Video – Lesson 16
Graphing Distance vs. Time (Same Speed, Different Starting Points)

Lesson 16 is another key lesson. Students graph objects with the same speed but different starting points. Bicyclists A, B, and C all travel at a rate of 5 mph. However, Bicyclist B has a 10-mile "head start," and bicyclist C has a 15-mile "head start."

In Box A, use d = rt (a proportion in disguise) to calculate the distance traveled. Graph the result.

In Box B, graph bicyclist B without performing any calculations. Since bicyclist B has a 10-mile head start, draw a point at the starting distance of 10 miles on the y-axis. The demo video points out that this **"head start"** is known as the **"y-intercept."**

Then, from the head start (y-intercept), continuously draw additional points by going up 5 miles and over 1 hour since the speed **(slope)** is 5 miles per hour.

At the end of the lesson, the demo video uses the formula d = rt to derive the formulas for each line, which are **y = 5x** for bicyclist A, **y = 5x + 10** for bicyclist B, and **y = 5x + 15** for bicyclist C. These are parallel lines with the same speed (slope) but different starting points, or head starts (y-intercepts).

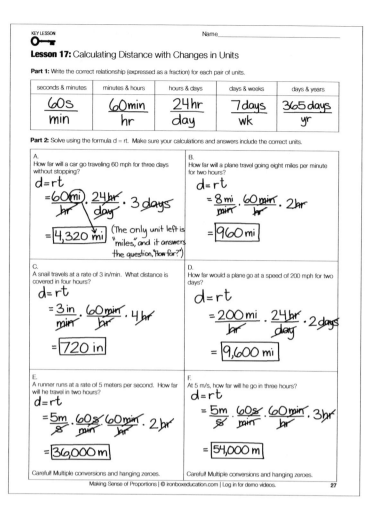

KEY LESSON

Name_____

Lesson 17: Calculating Distance with Changes in Units

Part 1: Write the correct relationship (expressed as a fraction) for each pair of units.

seconds & minutes	minutes & hours	hours & days	days & weeks	days & years
$\dfrac{60s}{min}$	$\dfrac{60min}{hr}$	$\dfrac{24hr}{day}$	$\dfrac{7\,days}{wk}$	$\dfrac{365\,days}{yr}$

Part 2: Solve using the formula d = rt. Make sure your calculations and answers include the correct units.

A. How far will a car go traveling 60 mph for three days without stopping?

$d = rt$

$= \dfrac{60\,mi}{hr} \cdot \dfrac{24\,hr}{day} \cdot 3\,days$

$= \boxed{4,320\,mi}$ (The only unit left is "miles," and it answers the question, "How far?")

B. How far will a plane travel going eight miles per minute for two hours?

$d = rt$

$= \dfrac{8\,mi}{min} \cdot \dfrac{60\,min}{hr} \cdot 2\,hr$

$= \boxed{960\,mi}$

C. A snail travels at a rate of 3 in/min. What distance is covered in four hours?

$d = rt$

$= \dfrac{3\,in}{min} \cdot \dfrac{60\,min}{hr} \cdot 4\,hr$

$= \boxed{720\,in}$

D. How far would a plane go at a speed of 200 mph for two days?

$d = rt$

$= \dfrac{200\,mi}{hr} \cdot \dfrac{24\,hr}{day} \cdot 2\,days$

$= \boxed{9,600\,mi}$

E. A runner runs at a rate of 5 meters per second. How far will he travel in two hours?

$d = rt$

$= \dfrac{5m}{s} \cdot \dfrac{60s}{min} \cdot \dfrac{60\,min}{hr} \cdot 2\,hr$

$= \boxed{36,000\,m}$

Careful! Multiple conversions and hanging zeroes.

F. At 5 m/s, how far will he go in three hours?

$d = rt$

$= \dfrac{5m}{s} \cdot \dfrac{60s}{min} \cdot \dfrac{60\,min}{hr} \cdot 3\,hr$

$= \boxed{54,000\,m}$

Careful! Multiple conversions and hanging zeroes.

Making Sense of Proportions | © ironboxeducation.com | Log in for demo videos. 27

Name_____

Lesson 18: Calculating Distance with Changes in Units

Part 1: Write the correct relationship (expressed as a fraction) for each pair of units.

seconds & minutes	minutes & hours	hours & days	days & weeks	days & years
$\dfrac{60s}{min}$	$\dfrac{60\,min}{hr}$	$\dfrac{24\,hr}{day}$	$\dfrac{7\,days}{wk}$	$\dfrac{365\,days}{yr}$

Part 2: Solve using the formula d = rt. Make sure your calculations and answers include the correct units.

A. How far will a plane go traveling 90 mph for three days without stopping?

$d = rt$

$= \dfrac{90\,mi}{hr} \cdot \dfrac{24\,hr}{day} \cdot 3\,days$

$= \boxed{6,480\,mi}$

B. How far will a plane travel going ten miles per minute for two hours?

$d = rt$

$= \dfrac{10\,mi}{min} \cdot \dfrac{60\,min}{hr} \cdot 2\,hr$

$= \boxed{1,200\,mi}$

C. A snail travels at a rate of 2 in/min. What distance is covered in five hours?

$d = rt$

$= \dfrac{2\,in}{min} \cdot \dfrac{60\,min}{hr} \cdot 5\,hr$

$= \boxed{600\,in}$

D. How far would a plane go at a speed of 100 mph for three days?

$d = rt$

$= \dfrac{100\,mi}{hr} \cdot \dfrac{24\,hr}{day} \cdot 3\,days$

$= \boxed{7,200\,mi}$

E. A runner runs at a rate of 6 meters per second. How far will he travel in two hours?

$d = rt$

$= \dfrac{6m}{min} \cdot \dfrac{60s}{min} \cdot \dfrac{60\,min}{hr} \cdot 2\,hr$

$= \boxed{43,200\,m}$

Careful! Multiple conversions and hanging zeroes.

F. A runner runs at a rate of 6 m/s. How far will he go in one hour?

$d = rt$

$= \dfrac{6m}{s} \cdot \dfrac{60s}{min} \cdot \dfrac{60\,min}{hr} \cdot 1\,hr$

$= \boxed{21,600\,m}$

Careful! Multiple conversions and hanging zeroes.

Making Sense of Proportions | © ironboxeducation.com | Log in for demo videos. 28

Key Points from Demo Video – Lesson 17
Calculating Distance with Changes in Units

In Lesson 17, students continue calculating distances, but now they have to work with changes in units that require conversions.

These types of problems can confound students to no end, so they will learn how to solve them more easily. The key to avoiding confusion is to include the units in your calculations. This way, the numerical values carry meaning, which helps you keep track of the logic.

In Part 1, students write the correct relationships (expressed as a fraction) for each pair of units. For example, the relationship between seconds and minutes is that there are 60 seconds in one minute, as shown in the answer key.

In Box A, the question asks how far a car will travel going 60 miles per <u>hour</u> for three <u>days</u> without stopping. Notice the change in units. The demo video shows how to use the relationships in Part 1 to convert units and easily solve the problems in Part 2.

Boxes E and F require multiple conversions to go from seconds to hours. There are 60 <u>seconds</u> per <u>minute</u>, and there are 60 minutes per <u>hour</u>.

Key Points from Demo Video – Lesson 18
Calculating Distance with Changes in Units

In Lesson 18, students continue calculating distances with changes in units that require conversions.

The key to avoiding confusion is to include the units in your calculations. This way, the numerical values carry meaning, which helps you keep track of the logic.

In Part 1, write the correct relationships (expressed as a fraction) for each pair of units. For example, there are 60 seconds in one minute, as shown in the answer key.

In Box A, the question asks how far a plane will travel going 90 miles per <u>hour</u> for three <u>days</u> without stopping. Notice the change in units. The demo video shows how to use the relationships in Part 1 to convert units and easily solve the problems in Part 2.

Boxes E and F require multiple conversions to go from seconds to hours. There are 60 <u>seconds</u> per <u>minute</u>, and there are 60 minutes per <u>hour</u>.

Name_____

Lesson 19: Calculating Distance with Changes in Units

Part 1: Write the correct relationship (expressed as a fraction) for each pair of units.

seconds & minutes	minutes & hours	hours & days	days & weeks	days & years
$\dfrac{60s}{min}$	$\dfrac{60min}{hr}$	$\dfrac{24hr}{day}$	$\dfrac{7\,days}{wk}$	$\dfrac{365\,days}{yr}$

Part 2: Solve using the formula d = rt. Make sure your calculations and answers include the correct units.

A.
A car on the freeway travels 90 feet per second. How far does it go in 5 seconds?

$d = rt$

$= \dfrac{90ft}{s} \cdot 5s$

$= \boxed{450\,ft}$

B.
How far will it go in 5 minutes?

$d = rt$

$= \dfrac{90ft}{s} \cdot \dfrac{60s}{min} \cdot 5\,min$

$= \boxed{27,000\,ft}$

C.
The Space Shuttle travels at a rate of 18,000 mph. How far does it go in three days?

$d = rt$

$= \dfrac{18,000\,mi}{hr} \cdot \dfrac{24hr}{day} \cdot 3\,days$

$= \boxed{1,296,000\,mi}$

D.
At three meters per second, what distance is covered by an athlete running for two hours?

$d = rt$

$= \dfrac{3m}{s} \cdot \dfrac{60s}{min} \cdot \dfrac{60min}{hr} \cdot 2\,hr$

$= \boxed{21,600\,m}$

Careful! Multiple conversions and hanging zeroes.

E.
A bird flies at a rate of 12 meters per second. How far will it go in 4 hours?

$d = rt$

$= \dfrac{12m}{s} \cdot \dfrac{60s}{min} \cdot \dfrac{60min}{hr} \cdot 4\,hr$

$= \boxed{172,800\,m}$

Careful! Multiple conversions and hanging zeroes.

F.
A bird flies at a rate of 4 meters per second. How far will it go in 8 hours?

$d = rt$

$= \dfrac{4m}{s} \cdot \dfrac{60s}{min} \cdot \dfrac{60min}{hr} \cdot 8\,hr$

$= \boxed{115,200\,m}$

Careful! Multiple conversions and hanging zeroes.

Making Sense of Proportions | © ironboxeducation.com | Log in for demo videos.   29

Key Points from Demo Video – Lesson 19
Calculating Distance with Changes in Units

In Lesson 19, students continue calculating distances with changes in units that require conversions.

Students should be especially careful with Box C since it involves many hanging zeroes in addition to the changes in units. As shown in the answer key, a Space Shuttle traveling at a rate of 18,000 miles per <u>hour</u> for three <u>days</u> travels 1,296,000 miles.

Boxes D, E, and F require multiple conversions to go from seconds to hours. There are 60 <u>seconds</u> per <u>minute</u>, and there are 60 minutes per <u>hour</u>.

Name_____

Lesson 20: Calculating Distance with Changes in Units

Part 1: Write the correct relationship (expressed as a fraction) for each pair of units.

seconds & minutes	minutes & hours	hours & days	days & weeks	months & years
$\dfrac{60s}{min}$	$\dfrac{60min}{hr}$	$\dfrac{24\,hr}{day}$	$\dfrac{7\,days}{wk}$	$\dfrac{12\,mo}{yr}$

Part 2: Solve using the formula d = rt. Make sure your calculations and answers include the correct units.

A.
A tree grows three inches per month. How much taller will it be in 4 years?

$d = rt$

$= \dfrac{3in}{mo} \cdot \dfrac{12mo}{yr} \cdot 4\,yr$

$= \boxed{144\,in}$

B.
A ship travels at a rate of 30 mph. How far will it go on a six day cruise?

$d = rt$

$= \dfrac{30mi}{hr} \cdot \dfrac{24hr}{day} \cdot 6\,days$

$= \boxed{4,320\,mi}$

C.
An arrow traveling 200 feet per second hits its target in three seconds. How far away is the target?

$d = rt$

$= \dfrac{200ft}{s} \cdot 3s$

$= \boxed{600\,ft}$

D.
A glacier travels 30 meters per day. How far does it travel in 3 weeks?

$d = rt$

$= \dfrac{30m}{day} \cdot \dfrac{7\,days}{wk} \cdot 3\,wk$

$= \boxed{630\,m}$

E.
At the equator, the earth rotates 25,000 miles in one day. How far does it rotate in two weeks?

$d = rt$

$= \dfrac{25,000\,mi}{day} \cdot \dfrac{7\,days}{wk} \cdot 2\,wk$

$= \boxed{350,000\,mi}$

Careful! Hanging zeroes.

F.
At the equator, the earth rotates 25,000 miles in one day. How far does it rotate in the month of April?

$d = rt$

$= \dfrac{25,000\,mi}{day} \cdot 30\,days$

$= \boxed{750,000\,mi}$

Careful! Hanging zeroes.

30   Making Sense of Proportions | © ironboxeducation.com | Log in for demo videos.

Key Points from Demo Video – Lesson 20
Calculating Distance with Changes in Units

In Lesson 20, students continue calculating distances with changes in units that require conversions.

These problems are actually easier compared to Lessons 17, 18, and 19 because none of them require multiple conversions. Box C requires no conversion at all. This gives students experiences with problems that require one conversion, multiple conversions, or no conversion at all.

Box A uses a unit relationship that has not yet been used in prior lessons. Students need to know that there are 12 <u>months</u> in one <u>year.</u>

Students should be careful with Box E, which uses many hanging zeroes.

Box F says that at the equator, the earth rotates 25,000 miles in one <u>day.</u> It asks, "How far does it rotate in the <u>month of April</u>?" Students need to know that there are 30 days in the month of April.

Making Sense of Proportions | © MathFluency.com | **Teachers: Log in for demo videos.**   41

Made in the USA
San Bernardino, CA
06 August 2018